The Phoenix Living Poets

———∞∞∞∞———

THE PAGODA
and Other Poems

The Phoenix Living Poets

★

ALEXANDER BAIRD: *Poems*
ALAN BOLD: *To Find the New*
A Perpetual Motion Machine
GEORGE MACKAY BROWN: *The Year of the Whale*
JENNIFER COUROUCLI: *On this Athenian Hill*
GLORIA EVANS DAVIES: *Words – for Blodwen*
PATRIC DICKINSON: *This Cold Universe*
The World I see
D. J. ENRIGHT: *Addictions · The Old Adam*
Some Men are Brothers · Unlawful Assembly
JOHN FULLER: *Fairground Music*
The Tree that Walked
DAVID GILL: *Men Without Evenings*
J. C. HALL: *The Burning Hare*
MOLLY HOLDEN: *To Make Me Grieve*
JOHN HORDER: *A Sense of Being*
P. J. KAVANAGH: *On the Way to the Depot*
RICHARD KELL: *Control Tower*
LAURIE LEE: *The Sun my Monument*
LAURENCE LERNER: *The Directions of Memory*
CHRISTOPHER LEVENSON: *Cairns*
EDWARD LOWBURY: *Time for Sale · Daylight Astronomy*
NORMAN MACCAIG: *Measures · A Round of Applause*
A Common Grave · Surroundings · Rings on a Tree
JAMES MERRILL: *Nights and Days · Selected Poems*
RUTH MILLER: *Selected Poems*
LESLIE NORRIS: *Finding Gold*
ROBERT PACK: *Selected Poems*
ARNOLD RATTENBURY: *Second Causes*
ADRIENNE RICH: *Selected Poems*
JON SILKIN: *Nature with Man*
The Re-ordering of the Stones
JON STALLWORTHY: *Root and Branch*
GILLIAN STONEHAM: *When that April*
EDWARD STOREY: *North Bank Night*
TERENCE TILLER: *Notes for a Myth*
SYDNEY TREMAYNE: *The Swans of Berwick*
LOTTE ZURNDORFER: *Poems*

THE PAGODA
and Other Poems
by
DAVID GILL

CHATTO AND WINDUS

THE HOGARTH PRESS

1969

Published by
Chatto and Windus Ltd
with The Hogarth Press Ltd
42 William IV Street
London W.C.2

★

Clarke, Irwin and Co Ltd
Toronto

SBN 7011 1536 X

PR
6057
.I54
P3

© David Gill 1969

Printed in Great Britain by
William Lewis (Printers) Ltd Cardiff

For Rene,
without whom . . .

Acknowledgements are due to the editors of the following periodicals and publications, in which some of the poems first appeared: *Breakthru, Country Life, Envoi, John O' London's Weekly, P.E.N. New Poems 1968, Transition, Twentieth Century, Unjustified* (Kent University), *Informer,* and B.B.C. *Midland Poets, The Poet's Voice.*

Contents

The Pagoda	9
On the Cathedral Floor	11
Kite	12
Merry-Go-Round	13
Beatrix Potter	14
Cézanne	15
October	16
He Sleeps	17
Buses	18
The Common	19
Pantomime	21
The Meadow	22
Cranes	24
Coming Across Zebras	25
Nests	26
Liberation	27
Killing a Whale	29
Krk	30
The Garden	31
The Home-coming	32
Adoption	33
Give and Take	34
Lucas Cranach's Adam and Eve – Magdeburg	35
Galileo Galilei	36
In Memory of George Sturt, Wheelwright	37
Tumuli	38
December 1960	39
Armistice-Day 1961	40
Nostalgia	41
Return to Bikini	42
Hué	44
Meditation in St. John's College Garden	47

Mohandas Gandhi and the Onion Pickers	49
Algiers 1962	50
For Dennis Brutus who was shot down while escaping from the South African Police	51
Grandfather	53

The Pagoda

Shouting, voice wide as the fields,
leapfrogging the hedges, wider,
fly-tickling pricked ears of cows munching horizons;

thick as thieves with the nimble-winged swallows
low-flying with tips for his ears,
signing with flourish a thousand times over

his contract for summer, my son
rides high at the top of his voice,
at vantage, head and shoulders above my head

and shoulders, hands buried deep
in the bunched-up reins of my hair.
As he jolts on the hump of my neck I remember

riding my Christopher father
fearless, enthroned without foothold,
across comparable fields, over stiles, under face-flipping twigs.

Photos there may be that show
my father mounted high
on financier shoulders among Edwardian clouds.

Like the circumflex roofs
of a pagoda, one perched on top
of the other, we children ride with eyes for the swallows:

also we gallop as fathers,
steeds for the conquest of summers,
bearing above us the shouts of our after-comers.

Standing, puffed, I see
that the strength of my pagoda
lies with me, penultimate storey — for I

remember the legend of founding,
roofed eras of growth, whilst my son
has not learned to remember and is gabled by sky.

On the Cathedral Floor

Flag-stones: cold, uneven, still abrasive.
Are hard on small impenitent hands and knees.
Fingers trace the worn, dirt-lined engravings,
poke the scars of chipped obituaries.

Bunches of angels hang from exploding branches
watching the aisles. Six hundred years below
my son makes progress on the gothic floor,
ant-explorer, crawling to and fro
between the massive trees.

Parallel bishops in slumbering robes of stone
float feet-first on draughts through the deathly apse;
straight crusaders spurning their bed-rock dogs
question the distant vaults and sense collapse

through broken noses. Now my son has found
a hymn-book. Stops among the monuments
to try the tensile strength of pious pages
beside the hardy bones of Saxon kings
who have not laughed for ages.

Kite

So here's another chance to fly a kite
for the wind has played the wildcat with our string.
My sons have lost their tempers with the thing,
demand solution. Could I help? I might.

It wriggles with each salty gust. I pin
it down, an all-in wrestler back to canvas,
and pick the wind-blown knots. The boys fizz up
and down. The wind is breathing. Let's begin.

Harlequin kite, did you want to dance with me
or flounder on my forearm like a shield?
But when with a hollow sigh away you reeled
between the bathing huts and up the quay

hugging the ball of Atlantic winds to your ribs,
you were man overboard, your ribboned pig-tail flying
and all your gay red courage thinly dying:
clinging, going, a goner, you diminished

until no bigger than a domino
you intimate by jerks your far-off dread
along this parabolic curve of thread.
How easy it would be to let you go!

But let's hold on. For kites we've always flown
from shingle beaches or from shaven downs,
and fathers steal the rituals of their sons
and fly their emblems as their very own.

Merry-Go-Round

Between the turning two antipodes
of makeshift sky and lately bolted boards
the golden horses spitted in their threes
sweep round on their predestined tracks.
The children cling like fruit to autumn trees,
taut-faced, a quick tangential smile thrown out
as round they come in threes, in leaping threes,
on snow-bound mounts caparisoned in gold,
and all the while the golden horses come,
the organ chews the cardboard melodies
and carved rococo bandgirls beat their drums.

But at the static centre of this fun,
glimpsed between flying tails and driving heads,
observe the engineer, a mournful rag
suspended from a loose forgotten hand,
a convict in the thrilling world he runs.

Beatrix Potter

Must hanker sometimes for a past
whose pillars stood and whose pilasters,
whose stucco ceilings still decant
their icy scorn on bed-and-breakfasters;
must hanker for a solid era
well-built behind the frail wisteria.

O bourgeois Kensington, I think
of frilly housemaids whitening thresholds,
the knots of nurses walking pink-
faced babes through squares of lyric thrushes,
the coachman in the mews, the queen
majestic, though seldom ever seen.

So golden was that golden age
her father scorned the working habit,
Miss Potter played behind the chintz
with handy mice and velvet rabbits;
her mother sewed; the plane-trees shed
their seeds; seldom was very much said.

So down her rabbit-hole she fled
to paint the cosy life of warrens:
the jacketed Bouncer bunnies bred
by simple genesis, a method foreign
to the usual manner of burrow sex —
but nothing was said on those aspects.

And yet into this four-inch world
an evil stalks with ears isoseles,
red whiskers and a suave paw curled
around a trigger. Mr Tod it is
who stores the bunnies in a sack,
who starts a Belsen in his shack.

Cézanne

Bent like a bracket on the mountain road,
dust and flies in his ragged beard,
easel on his back and like a cross
the unfinished canvas punishing the man,

Cézanne the ladder of shadows climbs.
Strange that on an evening such as this —
orange rocks, once mirrors
of the sun, bulk grey,

rhinoceros grey and cool as churches,
and caves of darkness shape beneath
the meditating chestnut trees,
and grapes swarm indolent and close —

strange that when the fitful bats
criss-cross the sky and mountain locked in truce
the testy painter finds no peace,

but unresolved and infinitely far
the dreamt-of final form, the colours
bite like sores into his back.

October

King Oedipus stepped briskly through the leaves,
October riding in his unshut eyes,
and all the leaves were whispering reprieves
for him the unreproached. But prophesies

wound horns for fear-meets in his memory.
He came upon sick children lobbing sticks
in careful cadence into a chestnut tree,
and conkers fell, and leaves like elegies.

He came upon brown nurses urging prams
across the park. They buckled at the breeze
and wheeled their tiny wistful anagrams
away to their solutions: destinies.

The sun withdrew sedately like a hearse,
and all the hope, the conkers and the children
seemed trivial assets in a bankrupt season:
they could not mask the aspect of the curse.

He Sleeps

He sleeps and sleeps as if no happening
would wake him. Shadows of chestnut leaves
point together and part like boats
in the pool of his lost inscrutable face.

From his dappled berth beneath the tree
He seems to concentrate in sleep,
fists clenched, on some leviathan –
some dream of panoramic sweep

including me, this book, this bench,
that old man crumbling charity
to sparrows, this path agog with girls
as sensitive to stares as flags

to brushing winds, and all the trees
and all the darting, jersied boys
in the park of cracking bats, the dumb
crusades of kites above the noise

of London's labours. His sleep projects
us all on focal lengths against
the summer day, and when he stirs,
the striving kites lose confidence

and hang upon their strings and sink . . .
But you who pass us by may see
a sleeping child no stronger than
a dot on some periphery.

Buses

The buses once had eyes and moved like masks
among the lamp-posts of the dreaming suburbs,
the buses red as poster-paints, the eyes
as big as dishes, tender eyes and troubled.
Small children wondered at these gentle looks
in life familiar from their story-books.

Each day they used to rise above the brow
and stagger red-faced to the almond tree
beside our gate, and stop. Somewhere I know
they used like patient mares dispersing flies
to shake off all vexations of the blitz
and on the all-clear roads collect their wits.

They came at night while search-lights carved the sky
to screaming joints of pain and children clung
to anaesthetic mothers who clung in turn
to shell-shocked providence. Their great eyes flung
in bold type terror at tottering masonry:
you knew it; you were never out to see.

I think the ad-men gave those buses eyes
to comfort London's children when among
the roofs a siren flew its moaning kite
and angry ogres shook the shelter-irons
and smelt the blood. Then from his shattered door
a child could see the buses as before.

On winter nights when silver moon-beams fell
like shrapnel on the unfleshed almond tree,
a staring bus would falter up the hill –
but one I never raised my head to see,
content to watch my frosted window-pane
slide round the room, and halt, and move again . . .

The Common

On earliest legs those walks across the common
Seemed endless; ended on my father's neck,
Who hunted the wood ant with the glossy brown abdomen
To study under glass in its social context.
The glades unfolded like the fawn savannahs,
Gorse-bushes round-backed lowered their thousand horns,
The yaffles there had the old derisive manners
And riddled the woods with bursts of rapid fire.
The silver-birches then in those silver noons
For all their slenderness and their threadbare stole
Of leaves could blot out flashes from the roads
And keep the dream of untouched common whole.

From days of villeinage to central-heated now
We've had the right to gather fallen faggots,
We had the ancient right to graze a cow
Or goat. We had no cows to graze, nor goats.
Instead we shared, unthreatened by enclosure,
All oaks converted into galleons and Troys,
Refought through cockpits and bogs campaigns of Caesar:
There reigned a socialism of little boys.
I recollect an order of events:
We heaped the biggest bonfire of the peace,
And next we saw through all the forest rents
The khaki lorries rolling to the east.

The bad time passed. Where once the guns had piped
Their shells into a Dornier-ridden night,
The sky was silent now, its approaches wiped
Clean for the birds. And boys and girls arrived
Taller from the chrysalids of their rough
Evacuated childhoods. The common had shrunk:
The red of buses shone through bright enough
To bleed each clump and glade of secrecy.
And when they walked among the trees as lovers

Later, the roar of motors wrapped its rope
Around them and top-deck eyes stole all the cover,
And owlwings only restored the lovers' hope.

Today the birches crown a traffic-island
On which no villager would care to graze his cow,
The common's privacy is something bygone
And public land — is really public now.

Pantomime

And only when the safety curtain slid
like a giant eye-lid to the magic stage
did we, the treated children, realise
that this was half-way through a phantom age,
and for the sweet duration of that blink
we were content in still parenthesis
to suck our wooden ice-cream spoons and think.

How can we ever recollect those weeks
of looking forward now as we sit at ease
in the upper circle half the pantomime through?
I know beneath the furry auspices
of aunts we almost dodged the German war,
and what if unwarned bombs fell should we do
and the whole balcony sagged like a broken jaw?

And once the interval had turned to dusk
with slow-dimmed lights, benighted in our seats,
we watched the ticking croc crunch buccaneer
and pat, we were out in the dazzling London streets.
But at least, as we left, we had no need to fear
the boy shut in the bubble of his youth
would be one thumb-length taller come next year.

The Meadow

A good wide meadow is something we all
can do with: an unploughed place where whatever winds
blow freely blow and where the utmost ripple
of ring-road zooming its tufted mile has thinned
to an insect bourdon; an unfenced place to recall
freedoms netted, chloroformed and pinned
on neat domestic cards; an interval
in which to set your pecking crow-cares free
and watch them shrink to white infinity.

This meadow, this fragment of prairie, puszta and plain,
this tiny savannah has all that sense of space
sewn in between the Thames and railway line.
How often I have halted face to face
with cropping cows and fancied the sniffed disdain
of buffaloes, or thought the horses of the place,
the chestnuts, hartebeests shyly trying to feign
the monumental still of termite-heaps:
a gathered strangeness makes the fancy leap.

But what of the white and the grey and the silver mares
that roam, not in herds, but each a beast
by itself, knee-deep through a yellow tide of flowers?
They let you come so near with but the least
lift of the nostril before their otherworldly stares
fix you to the spot, and you have ceased
to bridle them by eye as useful spares
to mend some worn-out symbol or ideal,
content to leave unbroken-in the real.

The herds stray freely unimpounded here,
among the cattle crass democracies
of geese flick up their rigid tongues to hiss
a Queen's own swan that navigates too near.
The history of the meadow is the history of these.

If once its hay was scythed by Cavalier
to feed his war-horse, once was cut to rear
frail bi-planes sketchy as mayflies into the air,
these human works of discipline were rare.

In the second month the animals recede
to higher ground while chill with melted snows
and grey the river's narrow crescent grows
to half-moon fatness in one night's feed.
Then sea-gulls come, the only unarked breed,
from starving coasts to colonise these rows
of shipwrecked elms; the primitive sun glows
on darkening pewter-greys. Go home and read:
this place has grown too lonely for your need.

Cranes

They must have shot section by section by starlight
when all of us in the shallow recession of sleep
slumbered half-hearing the clank at the window
but spurning until we drew the bright blinds
and knew that the cranes had struck at dawn.

And as we looked we saw the skyline
sink with its TV masts and chimneys,
the roof-tops humbled to knee-cap level
as the great cranes swung their giant elbows
creating space in the blue dimension.

The shadowy arms of their lofty business
cut the streets into birthday slices
and trawled us watchers together like sprats
in the mesh of their silent sweeping shadows
and cut us to size as we shielded our gaze.

But given a week, two weeks of the cranes
casting their hooks into unseen wells,
we all felt better, saluted the men
on the limb of the sky and acknowledged
that everywhere we were being uplifted

to live in the blue walls of exaltation
with swallows turning in airy lift-shafts
and skylarks singing the windows to bits
in attics where delicate angels sleep
on bales of softest cumulus cloud . . .

Coming Across Zebras

On Serengeti plains the golden stubble hums
and insects fuss among the droppings of the beasts
that fled to corrugate the skyline with their fear
and watch the mystic motor pass in veils of dust.

But we are real: the blood says yes, the sweat accuses.
The springs transmit the track's reality to real backsides,
but now rock softly as the silver thorns close in
and catch our view in mesh of frost and morningstars.

I touch you — but your hand is in the vision's glove.
All round us sparkle spikes and thorny asterisks,
and lovely living beyond the common scope of horses
the chevroned zebras twitch their silken rumps and gaze.

Nests

I'm looking for nests.
It's a mania. My eyes
flit sideways and upwards
picking the darkness of hedges.
The torn blue skies

hang through twigs.
And see, a dense
little blot of darkness
transfixed in a scribble of thorns!
Alone and intense

the detected nest
summons the curious mind
as ball calls hand.
What delicate treasures
will fingers find?

Luke-warm the eggs
all five like five
on a dice; though once
I would have stolen
and blown the life

of an unshaped bird
through a pin-hole, now
I'm content to go my way
reassured by the simple touch
my respect will allow.

Liberation

We are here in the blue-bell woods
To gather our soft tithes of flowers,
Which we when our memories touch them
Rediscover: their slippery stalks
And the manner their fleeting blue
Fades a shade in the fingers.

For him whose small hand fits
The socket of my fist
The woods are a bad dream of ogres
Enmeshed with the trees and the sky,
Where the sunlight flows round and gilds
The hair of their lumpish bodies,
While dragons chortle in maybush
At Martians with fishbowl heads,
And one-legged tree-giants bar
The paths with their sinewy toes.

A T.V. child of two years old
Is a bellowing zoo of monsters
That gnaw with quick teeth through their bars
And scatter howling for the trees
From which they dangle like spiders
All heavy, aggressive and golden.
His courage fails him. Don't
Let go his hand.

But give him a teazle
And he shouts like St. George:
Stingray will shoot you and kill you.
And down the squint-eyed ogres tumble
Flopping around us like skins of bananas
Their guts shot out.

I pick my bluebells ignoring the cries
Of whatever ogres repressed in my cells,
While he fills the forest with gunfire
And mops up the pockets of horror
Till the teazle slips from his fingers
And the woods are as free as the fields.

Killing a Whale

A whale is killed as follows:
A shell is filled with dynamite and
A harpoon takes the shell.
You wait until the great grey back
Breaches the sliding seas, you squint,
Take aim.
The cable snakes like a squirt of paint,
The shell channels deep through fluke
And flank, through mural softness
To bang among the blubber
Exploding terror through
The hollow fleshy chambers
While the hooks fly open
Like an umbrella
Gripping the tender tissue.

It dies with some panache
Whipping the capstan like
A schoolboy's wooden top
Until the teeth of the machine
Can hold its anger, grip.
Its dead tons thresh for hours
The ravished sea,
Then sink together, sag
So air is pumped inside
To keep the corpse afloat,
And one of those flags that men
Kill mountains with is stuck
Into this massive death.

Dead whales are rendered down,
Give oil.

Krk

Away from the mainland and its crises
your eyes give the full Adriatic response.
Our love is an absolute thing of the islands:
O open your eyes, and see once again —

The sun is a golden boy in the vines,
a ruthless lover of little red gardens.
As he dances from one orange roof to the next,
the bean plants twist to his music.

Already the harbour is an apron of green,
and a white boat is stitching a hem in the long
blue gown of the fish-woven sea beyond.
A cargo of melons is promised ashore.

D'you smell the new smell of fresh-baked bread?
Small children climb past us lugging their loaves.
Old women in the gardens like bits of charred paper
inspect the tomatoes and stoop over wells.

The sun is as mad as a girl's straw-hat
that flirts with the million walls of the island.
At mid-day we move to the cypress-tree's shade
or float like bottles in the cellars of the sea.

The island rocks in a golden hammock —
Who knows what voluptuous dreams it dreams?
I think the old crickets click naught but reproof
from their pulpits among the olive-tree leaves.

Your eyes are siestas of shuttered peace,
O love, let me in as they tenderly close.
The crickets are still; in the leaning shadows
Small stationary donkeys begin to doze.

The Garden

   Giant spiders, hair-legged and delicate,
     These are the sprinklers that tread
        The mossy clinker-beds, while in their wake

Wagtails fidgety as pressure-needles
   Flutter from knob to brittle knob.
     Flocks of seagulls stipple the razored lawns
A golfer's eye could take delight in,
   Which lie between the concrete channels
      Whence a faint smell conjures up the sea.

Within this strict renaissance landscape
   Sweet bacteria privily
      Purify the whole town's private poisons.

The Home-coming

. . . and by and by he came to Ithaca
despite the wayward winds and moody gods,
despite the Seven Seas' anathema:
his anchor dropped in face of endless odds.

And as he scanned the open, friendless shore
with flurried sea-gulls flaking from the cliff,
his pitching mind grew still: it seemed as if
his twenty years of sword and storm were more

than loyalty to Agamemnon's war,
were more than mounting into history
upon the cheated walls of Troy, were more
than trials of helmsmanship and mastery.

They were a prelude to this homeward hour
(for why he left was mainly to return)
and all the buoyant hours and steerboard days
were now mere tensions in his memory
bequeathing him a sovereign sense of power.

At last the will of him was flexed and free
to kill two decades' absence in one blow.
A vision came of pale Penelope.
He sprang ashore, craned like an iron bow.

Adoption

These pregnant days drag by with stitch in side
till we lose hope the hour will ever come
when our dark daughter, born for empty hands,
will now with no new ache be born for us.

We labour for you, mother and father both,
dark baby of my sonnet without rhyme:
these arms which held you once in that grey room
are worked into a cradle for you now,
and these white faces which your tongue-tip mocked
are still in this same world, will come again,
though they be lost as sunken stars at noon.

Among their files and three-fold documents
God's deputies dispose of you, of us —
and for your cradle rock a pending-tray.

Give and Take

Don't stop her now: her sucking lips take all,
control the long lax flow of milk
which runs in rivulets to every reach
where she may grow.

And while she drinks her eyes play back what's there:
Two polyphotos of my face
engraved with a settled seriousness
more candid for her candid stare
expressing nothing for her but
the only sureness left —
a shape of love.

My faces shock me from her own dark mirrors.
What am I to teach as one who ought to know?
About the first things and the last
what shall I say?

Thank God there is no need to tell her yet
that questions are an empty teat
through which no answers flow.
But meanwhile she has not yet broken faith
with the first things we have lost.
Still sure of something turning to respond
she tugs upon her rope of milk.

Lucas Cranach's Adam and Eve — Magdeburg

And all for an apple.
Two hands clasp the fruit
Which is whole but obviously doomed.
Already their slender bodies
Stretched by desire, yet parted by fear,
Shape a gracious urn in the trembling air between.
The placid deer among the leaves
See nothing of the virgin's fall of flesh
So swan-like sweeping from
The faintly punctuated breast
To the firmly pointed foot,
See nothing in the offing.
O Eve, you shopkeeper's daughter,
We can see from your sharp little chin
That you know what you want,
Where to get it.
Brown Adam with a head of golden curls
And wispy beard, looks shy,
Would like to back out
But not loth to go on
For as you see, the leafy twig
He holds so carefully
Conceals both nodes of generation:
Already he conceives in sin.

Galileo Galilei

For nothing, all for nothing the leaning Pisan swore
the studied facts were false, on rueful knees
before the established cardinals. Consider the score
of humiliation, fear and cowardice,

of failure to defend before the torturer's tools
the data of telescopes, precedence of eye
and brain. Autonomy of knowledge (maxim for our schools)
he was not martyr-made to justify.

For victims stir our hearts when what they stand and fall
for makes a difference. Had he been straight
and died for science' sake I doubt we would at all
have gained much from the sharpening of his fate.

We now gaze through the backward telescope of time
and see the Pisan's lie could not assuage
the manic tidal wave of progress nor the crime
which bursts in atoms on this frightened age.

In Memory of George Sturt, Wheelwright

The sinews of tradition sang all down
your arms unloading planks of chosen elm
for waggons in the chip and saw-dust realm
of knotty craftsmen. Knowing eyes would frown

the warps and shakes, all imperfections out
of naked wood, and at the hand's appeal
the felloes fused and spokes would sprout
from seasoned stock to flower: a waggon-wheel.

And then through England's lanes the spell-bound tree
would round its hub revolve a century.
And so perfection, wheelwright, spins for me –

the felled dreams lie across the tangled mind,
the bark of images is stripped to show
the dead-straight grain of relevance behind,
and soon the jobbing words begin the slow

and careful fashioning of stalwart verse,
the hub smooth-hewn, long-pondered, strong enough
to bear the overloads in rut and rough
till night defaces every artifice.

Tumuli

I think of the cold wind blowing the grassy scalps
Of the lonely tumuli;
I feel the razor-wind scraping the naked chalk
Of the sepulchres by the sea.

I draw my duffle-hood up and shiver inside
When I think of the tumuli
Heaped hundreds of years on the brow of the down
In sight of the immigrant sea.

The sleepers asleep with their potsherds, brooches and pins
Still live the slow life of the bone.
The wind which burns the flesh of my itinerant face
Leaves the soundly buried alone.

Sleep on in your wind-swept barrows! May no spade jar
Your iron-age reverie,
For your sons are digging new graves for themselves
And the cadaver of history.

Sleep on, uncultured fathers, whilst the tireless wind
Irradiates cold fears,
And if you may choose your resurrection hour,
Delay it — for a hundred years.

December 1960

Away across the brown clay fields
where thin silver lakes line the furrows
left by the slewing tractors yesterday,
to the backcloth of timeless manorial woods
there is little to mark this modern December
from those in our ancient calendars,
in ducal books of hours, in Flemish landscapes
and wintery tapestries rotting in faded castles.

Why, even the magpies which I see
like fragments of chess-board
balancing on posts in the mud of the field
are persistant remnants of a quiet past —
stick-in-the-mud emblems
of slow, rain-sodden, mediaeval winters.

Today my little moon-faced son sits in my lap
and stares past all the detail that I see.
For his sake I would wish this winter innocent —
mediaeval, slow, not ominous, not now.

Armistice-Day 1961

I have broken free, warm-coated, from my hearth.
The wind roves like a lancer through the beeches
And the copper leaves pour down the sighing lanes.
I shuffle along, discontented with the day,
Amazed at the holocaust I brush aside
With each disposing step. No armistice
Reins in the champing wind: the severed leaves
Twitch and fret in the mind like the dry statistics
Of all those dead brigades.
                      But I'm disloyal
To their sacrifice beneath the sour skies.
Like the poets of China who from their sleepy hovels
Scolded the dynasties for their ceaseless wars,
Resigned like that and sceptical of progress
I have lost my taste for noble sacrifice.
Was anything achieved? The winds today blow colder . . .
From the alms-houses where retired soldiers live, the smoke
Scrawls rapidly across the papery sky,
And last chrysanthemums duck their unkempt heads
Imparting a little sadness.

Nostalgia

I love old simple concepts you can wear
Like abbot's robes pinched by a single cord,
I should like to forget that things occurred
To crack the crystal of the ptolemaic spheres.

I see myself, a prying human, tear
A hole in Heaven's vault of stuck-on stars
And gaze at that divine machine which steers
The lucky universe to peace through war.

But now the earth is cut adrift and soars,
Flinging its people like hysterical hair,
And Heaven is a skull-cap or a lair
Of light-years lost beyond the star-lagged shore.

And yet this cosmic blind-man's buff I'd bear
If peace were final now as final war.

Return to Bikini

We wade through the wrinkling shallows
Which are lucid and lap the gay fish in garments of glass,
The fallow waves follow
Through the dead-white sculpture of coral
And sigh where their silence must break on the sand.

An island of silence —
Above the flowering grasses, the flowering trees
The bomb-shocked palms wave their idiot heads
Nodding together at evil recalled, lifting
At whisperings from the sea.

And now our lead-lined boots sink in the sand
And as our stony shapes advance
The birds go wild in the vivid trees:
Red bishops dart, green parrots swoop,
Blue starlings burst like splintered shale.

Go carefully now. Put everything to the test.
Just listen to the silence of the pebbles first.
The pebbles have little to say. The razor-shells
Say nothing. O taciturn limpets,
Your tongue-tied nil appeases . . .

Knock-knock, knock-knock,
The hermit-crabs urge from their shells,
Have confessions to make in the geiger-box:

"We are the trustees, we alone,
We are the enduring agents of decay,
We are the living isotopes
Reviving as we radiantly decease
The golden memory of how you altered all.
But what you did was not the end for us —
We are the anchorites of hope

And hope is the greatest lure
To tempt you on who see
The atolls green."

Hué

I

I speak of the golden peace of buddhist Vietnam,
a pervasion of incense in lofty pagodas.
A shaven monk goes small in sandalled silence
along the eight-fold path of wise Gautama's
or rests upon his heels before a fountain
fixing his emptying mind on the nozzle
whence the water willows up and catches bending
the kisses of light, descending
into the shallow basin of sky which overruns
all round to lock its slender stand
in a glittering prison . . .
I think of the wind-ruffled shawls of delicate roses
flung over the shoulders of the courtyard wall.
When the hollow gong drones in the inner temple
the monk's eye returns to the roses, the worldly.

II

Little monk, I think of your inward voyage
beneath a saffron sail from the shores
of clay and fire. I know you evade me
as the taste of lichees evades the tongue.
You will have, my antithesis, no eyes for roses,
no eyes for fair women or any flowers.
Your fetters lie in fragments in the dust
like severed snakes. A certain gravity
your soul outgrew, now floating free,
the anchors of desire abandoned,
you are the dumb moth hunting the quiet light,
the beacon of nothing in nowhere.

The pain, the suffering was always there.
The great wheel turning always groaned,

but now those forest sanctuaries
the hermits chose to crowd with prayers
are torn with the rage of bombs; the villages
burn, their dead are bits of jig-saw
mosaic among their shattered pots.
And when the snarling birds come low across the rice
and when the great pagodas fall
like playing-card towers blown down in pique,
what then, my monk, my moth?

III

The quietists fold up their dreams,
they tear up their robes to make saffron flags.
(O splendid flags!)
They take to the streets. With proclamations
they rouse the people.
The streets of Hué are full of the family altars,
the personal buddhas squat
like pyramids of golden peaches.

Can the innocence of dolls divert a tank?

Now weep in the temple of your wounds,
you are yourself the inevitable pain:
you acted, were forced to act, and so
in a world of suffering you chose your own.

IV

Sleep, my buddhist, it's time to sleep,
rest your head on these blooded robes.
Another hand will turn your prayer-wheel,
or if there is none, the wind will turn it.

Sleep is the basket from which your dreams
step out like beautiful doves,

fly up like a fountain, wheel about
and strike for Nirvana.

Meditation in St. John's College Garden

Here I want to raise my voice but do not
lest the steward trees choke off my words
and haul them heckling to their leafy prisons
to lose them in the hubbub of the birds.

Here the gardening centuries have turned this
place into a pleasance where the flowers
delight at every bending of the path and
scholars, thumb in page, footnote their hours.

All is raked and dunged, pruned and tended,
all for the schoolman's comfort. On the path
a bench bequeathed by some dead don,
a rock-garden there: its maker's epitaph.

What of the bitter winds that tear their sleeves on
teeth of broken glass along the wall
and what of slogans dragging their coiling letters
of blood across the world-face of those stones?

Candled chestnuts, elegant beeches neatly
interpose their beauty and their quiet.
This watch-committee of surly sandstone faces
has never beheld a barricade or riot.

Have you no martyrs whose ghosts might infiltrate the
lilac-trees and tremble there? Has all
reverie of violence been expelled from here and
left to rot unseen outside the wall?

Will you not think, you gentle theologians,
of what has been expunged from these calm walks?
The buddhist priests bleeding in burning pagodas,
and clouds of helicopters hanging like hawks.

No, ignore. For comfort, for your comfort
sit inside the chamber of this weeping beech
and ponder God. The garden-walls will serve to
keep the nailing easterlies at bay.

Mohandas Gandhi and the Onion Pickers
– a parable for the Committee of 100

Mohandas Gandhi, third-class traveller on Imperial trains
first picked the locks of shackled peasants with a safety pin.
Mohandas Gandhi, bare-legged as the labourers
walked nimbly through the dust of India's grievances.
Mohandas Gandhi, the mahatma, raised the eyes
of the indigo-pickers of Champeran to the forgotten hills
of self-esteem; he drove the gentle elephant
of justice through the court-rooms, breaking furniture,
apologizing in advance not afterwards.
Mohandas Gandhi fed the thirsty continent
from the melted snows of his Himalayan heights of
    conscience.

Now why did all the peasants in Kheda district cheer
when Mohanlal Pandya, disciple of Mohandas Gandhi,
and eight good friends plucked onions in the punishing sun?
They cheered because the government had seized the crop
to pay for revenue poor peasants would not pay;
they cheered at dusk when all the illicit roots were pulled
and when the laughing onion-thieves were led away
the peasants cheered again, and in the solemn court
they cheered the culprits and the magistrate next day.
When Mohandas Gandhi saw his followers again
he said: You have drawn the stubborn roots of the people's
    fear,
who knows what onions we may one day have to pick?
When men go cheerfully to gaol, repression loses heart.

Algiers 1962

We throb, the felt screws chewing the leagues
of voyage from level sea, and the white bows hew
the standard waves to fissured marble, flowers
of foam dilating after. Smoky blue,
the skyline spares us much

till now, at nightfall, the manifold portholes stare
at the city famous in broadcasts and weekly newsreels:
Algiers. The concrete tenements, step by step,
ascend the Muslim hills. A mosque protrudes
like a forthright thumb. Perhaps

the green flags flutter? From the reconciling sea
the streets which shadowed death in doorways, hate
in balconies, seem still. No sub-machine guns state
their unselective spleen, no bombs explode —
as if a milder fate

presided over the city and the bay
and you could make-believe the communiques
had furthered a fiction, made conflict and horror
from no such stuff. For cities are wonderfully healed,
the deep wounds hidden.

For Dennis Brutus who was shot down while escaping from the South African Police

Verwoerd's huge web no longer shakes. A hole
In the prisoner's stomach leaves him usefully prone.
O here, sir, is the usual plaster, stick the strips
Criss-cross on the poet's lips
And crucify this voice.

They would not say in the diamond cities,
Nor even breathe in the evening bars
That justice must define men equally
As black shapes white, white black
On the board where chessmen ape
Our larger politics.

He spoke when other voices trailed away
Migrating in the dusk, and laid his mines
On the open page, igniting the itching fuse
Of fizzing syllables, each stick of verse
An age of singing sabotage.

The wrong he saw crouched blindly in despair
Or screamed from brutal cells. No voice,
No knowing voice was there but his to hail
The alien world of friends
And draw a saving sail.

And so he went, the true words locked inside
His unpermitted head, to fall
Precisely headlong over rubber-stamping boots
Of frontier-police who pushed him back again,
For policemen here policemen there
They love policemen everywhere.

Policemen don't love poets who in general are
Disorderly and stir men up. So he

On instinct fled their uncongenial company.
He could not melt into the crowd: the crowd
Shrank back to let him and his hunters
And the hurting bullet through.
And only then Johannesburg threw up its blinds
To hear his strangled voice.

Grandfather

We came to speak of him as evening winds
Washed scents of beach and tar and tackle through
The avenues and crescents of this town
Retiring tete a tete with sea and downs,
To mingle with the perfumed crew of roses
Which he, land-lubberly at last, put down
To anchor his nostalgic eyes. Across
The many bowling-greens the trident shadows
Pricked their captains creaking home. And now
We came to speak of him, his daughter young
At sixty speaking chiefly, and myself.

"He ran away to sea, you know, a lad
Of seventeen, grew tough beneath the sail,
The sun, the discipline of wind and tide.
The world whose harbours, wharves and jetties knew
The quick impatient cast of rope he threw
Hid little from his coolly navigating gaze.
Once wrecked upon a freckle of an island
In the Southern Seas (the skipper whisky-blind
Had flung his hated ship like a wieldy wrestler
On a teething floor of rocks) my father learnt
That mastery of the ocean meant that first
One must become the master of oneself."

"But was he always master of himself?"

"At home not always, but I do recall
The jovial kindness of him and the fun
When after months of absence he would stride
Dark as mahogany into our laughing house.
For all of us he'd ransacked shrill bazaars:
For Jack he brought carved figurines,
An Arab flute for Frank, and for the girls
Stuffed camels, dolls and stools and scarves and fans

And Persian amber rings and Turkish Delight.
O how we gorged ourselves on sticky lumps
Of jellied paradise. And mother there
Submitting the log of all our good performances
But few of the bad with such a tender smile.
Her stringent watch expired when he came home;
For whilst *his* keel slit up the Persian Gulf
Or drowsed in the turquoise harbours of Japan,
Our mother single-handed steered us all
Through the teen-age straits of Leytonstone.

"But father came into his own again
When his trembling masts and scarlet funnel topped
The hunched grey dock-side houses, and he came
Ashore, his seaman's treasure-chest in train.
And every moment, so it seemed to us,
He grew until the branches of his laughter
Filled the house and shook the tiles like leaves.
How strong he was, our father! We used to hang
From his great arms and neck like pears and plums,
The baby athwart the crosstrees of his nape
Clutching the two royal ensigns of his ears.

"With us, he was jack of one trade: our whole-hearted
    father.
At sea he had a dozen ministries:
He sailed his state along the charted line,
He cured the sick with mixtures from a chest,
And broken limbs he set unflinchingly
With skill; the dead he buried with a homely prayer.
And there were times when he who shared a deck
With Conrad once found life outstripping seayarns.
Not many miles off Singapore, one close
And listless afternoon, a lascar flew
Berserk. With sharp little screams of senseless rage,
A long knife twitching in his fist, he drove

His mates like rats below the bolted decks.
Then, alone, confused and fetching froth
He drooped, panting beneath the captain's bridge.
And then our father sprang: like an iron press
He pinned the furious epileptic to the deck."

"He must have been a tough resourceful man,
Though I still see a gentle Gandhian face,
A little shrivelled, roundish, Bedouin-brown,
The plum-red dressing-gown, the towering bed. ."

"Yes, that was near the end. The tough old man
Grew weak, irascible as old efficiences
Broke down, abandoned him upon the beach
Of illness beyond the sea's condolences."

"His moods, I'm told, were terrible to see."

"His temper billowed like a broad, slack sail
Distended by a sudden hurricane
Which struck and drove him into cruel complaints,
But just as swiftly set him free again."
She smiled and went on softly, "When the house
Is still, the night outside glows orange with
The sodium lamps, the cars have gone, and I
Am by myself, I sense that he is here,
About this house, held back by love, remorse,
The whole deep-anchored aptitude he had
For living fully, fiercely, always fatherly."
She paused: "Perhaps he's in this very room
Filling his pipe, inclined, and listening to us.
That telescope under his arm, he may be on
The stairs, regaining breath. Or then, again
He may be standing by your son's divan
Searching the tiny chart of the baby's face
For some remote resumption of his own."